VALERIA MOORE

AI for ALL

How AI can enhance the lives of everyday individuals

This book was professionally typeset on Reedsy.
Find out more at reedsy.com

"In the vast tapestry of the cosmos, woven with the threads of human curiosity, lies the promise of endless discovery. As we journey deeper into the realms of knowledge, guided by the light of innovation, we encounter the wondrous creations of our own making, where artificial intelligence serves as both architect and muse, illuminating the path to a future yet to be imagined."

- Unknown

Contents

1 Introduction   1

2 Definition of AI & Generative AI - A brief history   2

3 The impact of AI in Healthcare   10

4 AI contribution to Education   14

5 The Influence of AI on Employment and the Workplace   18

6 The power of AI on the Finance Industry   22

7 How AI is Reshaping Transportation   26

8 Smart Cities: Enhancing Urban Living through AI Integration   30

9 AI and Social Interaction   33

10 Ethical Considerations and Challenges   36

11 Future Trends   38

12 Conclusion: Navigating the Future Landscape of AI   40

1

Introduction

I n the era of AI, where information overload and internet hype often lead to confusion, I recognized the need for a clear understanding of what AI truly is and its imminent impact on our daily lives. Despite my 30 years in technology, my grasp of AI was very basic. Intrigued by the potential applications and direct implications of AI on aspects like family, work, and personal life, I embarked on a journey to demystify this complex technology.

Drawing upon curiosity and my technology background, I set out to create a non-technical guide, steering away from the intricacies of coding and algorithms. Instead, I aimed to offer a simple exploration of AI, providing basic definitions and practical applications that resonate with everyday experiences.

This book is not geared towards tech enthusiasts or industry experts. If you find yourself navigating the landscape of AI, seeking a comprehensible guide that unveils its significance in your life, then this book is tailored just for you. Join me in unraveling the transformative impact of AI and discovering how it shapes the world around us.

2

Definition of AI & Generative AI - A brief history

Artificial Intelligence (AI) refers to the capability of a machine or computer system to perform tasks that typically require human intelligence. These tasks include learning, reasoning, problem-solving, perception, language understanding, and even, to some extent, decision-making. AI systems are designed to mimic cognitive functions associated with human intelligence and, in some cases, surpass human capabilities in specific domains.

There are two main types of AI:

1. Narrow or Weak AI: This type of AI is designed and trained for a particular task. It excels at that specific task but lacks the broad cognitive abilities of a human. Examples include virtual personal assistants like Siri or Alexa, and image recognition software.
2. General or Strong AI: This refers to AI systems with the ability to understand, learn, and apply knowledge across various domains—similar to human intelligence. Achieving true general AI remains a theoretical and futuristic goal, and current AI systems are consid-

ered narrow or weak AI.

Key components and techniques within AI include:

- Machine Learning (ML): A subset of AI that involves the development of algorithms that enable systems to learn from data and improve their performance over time without explicit programming.
- Natural Language Processing (NLP): The ability of a computer system to understand, interpret, and generate human language in a way that is both meaningful and contextually relevant.
- Computer Vision: The capacity of a machine to interpret and make decisions based on visual data, often through the analysis of images or videos.
- Expert Systems: AI systems designed to mimic the decision-making abilities of a human expert in a particular domain by using predefined rules and knowledge.
- Robotics: The integration of AI and physical machines to create systems capable of performing tasks in the physical world.

AI applications are diverse, ranging from recommendation systems and autonomous vehicles to medical diagnosis and language translation. As technology continues to advance, the scope and impact of AI on various industries and aspects of daily life are expected to expand significantly.

Generative AI refers to a type of artificial intelligence system that is designed to generate content autonomously. Unlike traditional AI systems that are task-specific and operate within predefined boundaries, generative AI has the ability to create new and original content across various domains.

One notable form of generative AI is GPT (Generative Pre-trained

Transformer) models, like OpenAI's GPT-3. These models are pre-trained on vast amounts of diverse data and can generate human-like text based on prompts given to them. Generative AI can be applied to tasks such as natural language processing, image generation, music composition, and more, making it a versatile tool for creative and content-related applications.

A Brief History of Artificial Intelligence (AI)

The concept of Artificial Intelligence (AI) has deep historical roots, stretching back centuries, but the formal pursuit of creating intelligent machines began in the mid-20th century. Here's a condensed overview of the key milestones in the development of AI:

Ancient Dreams and Automata (Antiquity - 19th Century):

- The idea of creating artificial beings with human-like capabilities dates back to ancient civilizations. Mythical tales often depicted the creation of automatons and artificial life.
- In the 17th century, mathematician and philosopher René Descartes proposed the idea of animal-like machines, arguing that non-human animals could be explained as biological machines.

Emergence of Computing (1930s - 1940s):

- The theoretical foundations of computation were laid by mathematicians such as Alan Turing and Alonzo Church in the 1930s. Turing's conceptualization of a universal machine set the stage for modern computers.
- During World War II, computers were developed for code-breaking purposes, providing practical applications for theoretical ideas.

Birth of AI (1950s – 1960s):

- The term "Artificial Intelligence" was coined by computer scientist John McCarthy in 1955 during the Dartmouth Conference, marking the formal beginning of AI as a field of study.
- McCarthy, along with Marvin Minsky, Nathaniel Rochester, and Claude Shannon, founded the Dartmouth Summer Research Project on Artificial Intelligence in 1956, considered the birth of AI as a discipline.
- Early AI research focused on symbolic reasoning, problem-solving, and learning.

Symbolic AI and Expert Systems (1960s – 1980s):

- Symbolic AI, also known as "Good Old-Fashioned AI" (GOFAI), dominated this era. Researchers aimed to represent human knowledge in symbolic form and create systems that could manipulate these symbols.
- Expert systems, designed to emulate human expertise in specific domains, gained prominence. MYCIN, developed in the 1970s, was an early example used for medical diagnosis.

AI Winter (1980s – 1990s):

- Unrealistic expectations, coupled with limited computing power, led to a period known as "AI Winter." Funding for AI research declined, and there was skepticism about the feasibility of achieving human-level intelligence in machines.
- Despite setbacks, research continued in areas like machine learning and neural networks.

Rise of Machine Learning (2000s – Present):

- Advances in computing power, the availability of vast datasets, and breakthroughs in algorithms fueled the resurgence of AI.
- Machine learning, particularly deep learning, gained prominence. Neural networks with multiple layers demonstrated remarkable capabilities in image recognition, natural language processing, and other complex tasks.

AI in the 21st Century:

- AI applications have become integral to various aspects of daily life, including virtual assistants, recommendation systems, autonomous vehicles, and healthcare diagnostics.
- Ongoing research explores the ethical implications of AI, addressing issues such as bias in algorithms and the impact of AI on employment.

The history of AI is a dynamic narrative of scientific breakthroughs, technological advancements, and societal shifts. As AI continues to evolve, its impact on various industries and aspects of human life is expected to deepen and diversify.

Importance of AI in daily life

The importance of Artificial Intelligence (AI) in daily life has grown exponentially, touching almost every aspect of our existence. From simplifying routine tasks to revolutionizing industries, AI has become an integral part of contemporary living. Here are key areas where AI significantly impacts and enhances our daily lives:

Personal Assistants and Smart Devices

- AI-driven personal assistants like Siri, Alexa, and Google Assistant have become ubiquitous, helping users manage schedules, answer queries, and perform various tasks using natural language processing.
- Smart devices, such as thermostats and lighting systems, use AI to learn user preferences, optimizing comfort and energy efficiency.

Communication and Language Translation

- AI facilitates seamless communication by enabling real-time language translation through applications like Google Translate.
- Chatbots powered by AI enhance customer support, responding to inquiries and resolving issues in a timely manner.

Entertainment and Content Recommendations

- Streaming services employ AI algorithms to analyze user preferences and behavior, offering personalized content recommendations.
- AI is used in the gaming industry to create more immersive experiences, adapting gameplay based on individual player behavior.

Healthcare and Medical Diagnosis

- AI plays a crucial role in medical image analysis, aiding in the early detection of diseases through technologies like computer-aided diagnostics.
- Personalized medicine benefits from AI algorithms that analyze genetic data to tailor treatment plans based on individual patient profiles.

7

Education and Learning

- AI in education supports personalized learning experiences, adapting to individual student needs and pacing.
- Intelligent tutoring systems use AI to provide real-time feedback, helping students strengthen their understanding of subjects.

E-commerce and Online Shopping

- AI-powered recommendation engines enhance the online shopping experience by suggesting products based on user preferences and browsing history.
- Chatbots in e-commerce platforms offer instant assistance, guiding users through the purchase process and addressing queries.

Transportation and Autonomous Vehicles

- AI contributes to improved transportation systems, optimizing traffic flow and predicting congestion patterns.
- The development of autonomous vehicles aims to enhance road safety and efficiency, reducing accidents caused by human error.

Finance and Fraud Detection

- AI is utilized in financial institutions for fraud detection, analyzing transaction patterns to identify potentially suspicious activities.
- Robo-advisors leverage AI algorithms to provide personalized financial advice and manage investment portfolios.

Workplace Productivity

- AI tools streamline business processes, automating repetitive tasks and freeing up human resources for more strategic and creative endeavors.
- Collaboration platforms use AI for natural language processing, facilitating communication and information retrieval.

Social Media and Content Creation

- AI algorithms power content curation on social media platforms, presenting users with content tailored to their interests.
- Creative tools, such as AI-generated art and music, demonstrate the potential for AI in artistic expression.

As AI technologies continue to advance, their integration into daily life is poised to deepen, providing solutions to existing challenges and creating new opportunities for convenience, efficiency, and innovation. However, ethical considerations, transparency, and responsible AI development are crucial to ensuring that AI benefits society as a whole.

Now, let's delve into a more comprehensive discussion about the various facets of our lives experiencing significant positive impacts from AI. These include healthcare, education, employment, finance, transportation, smart cities, and social interactions.

3

The impact of AI in Healthcare

The impact of Artificial Intelligence (AI) in healthcare has been transformative, revolutionizing various aspects of the industry. Here are key ways in which AI is making a significant difference in healthcare:

Medical Imaging and Diagnostics

- **Radiology and Pathology:** AI algorithms assist radiologists and pathologists in interpreting medical images, improving accuracy and speed in diagnosing conditions such as cancer, fractures, and abnormalities.
- **Early Detection:** AI enables the early detection of diseases by analyzing medical images, contributing to more timely and effective treatments.

Personalized Medicine

- **Genomic Analysis:** AI algorithms analyze large datasets of genetic information, helping identify genetic markers and tailor treatment plans based on individual patient profiles.

- **Drug Discovery:** AI accelerates drug discovery processes by predicting potential drug candidates, optimizing molecular structures, and identifying potential side effects.

Predictive Analytics and Risk Stratification

- AI models analyze patient data to predict disease progression, readmission risks, and potential complications, allowing healthcare providers to intervene proactively.
- Risk stratification helps prioritize resources and interventions for patients who are at higher risk of adverse health events.

Virtual Health Assistants and Chatbots

- AI-powered virtual assistants and chatbots provide real-time support and information to patients, answering queries, scheduling appointments, and offering guidance on medications and treatment plans.
- These tools enhance patient engagement and facilitate more efficient healthcare communication.

Clinical Decision Support Systems

- AI assists healthcare professionals in making informed decisions by providing evidence-based recommendations and relevant clinical information.
- Decision support systems help reduce errors, improve diagnostic accuracy, and enhance overall patient care.

Remote Patient Monitoring

- AI enables the continuous monitoring of patients with chronic conditions through wearable devices and sensors.
- Remote monitoring helps healthcare providers track patient health in real-time, intervene when necessary, and reduce the need for frequent hospital visits.

Administrative Efficiency

- AI streamlines administrative tasks, such as billing, scheduling, and record-keeping, reducing the burden on healthcare staff and improving overall operational efficiency.
- Automation of administrative processes allows healthcare professionals to focus more on patient care.

Drug Dosage Optimization

- AI algorithms assist in determining optimal drug dosages based on individual patient characteristics, reducing the risk of adverse reactions and improving treatment efficacy.
- Personalized dosage recommendations enhance the safety and effectiveness of medications.

Natural Language Processing (NLP) for Clinical Documentation

- NLP technology helps convert unstructured clinical notes into structured data, making it easier for healthcare providers to access and analyze patient information.
- Improved documentation enhances communication between healthcare professionals and supports data-driven decision-making.

Public Health Surveillance

- AI contributes to monitoring and predicting public health trends by analyzing large datasets, such as social media posts, electronic health records, and environmental factors.
- Early detection of disease outbreaks and tracking health trends at a population level is crucial for effective public health interventions.

While the impact of AI in healthcare is overwhelmingly positive, challenges such as data privacy, ethical considerations, and the need for regulatory frameworks must be carefully addressed to ensure responsible and equitable integration of AI technologies in healthcare practices.

4

AI contribution to Education

The impact of Artificial Intelligence (AI) in education is profound, reshaping the way students learn, teachers instruct, and educational institutions operate. Adaptive learning platforms use AI algorithms to tailor educational content based on individual student progress, ensuring that each learner receives a customized and effective educational journey. Here are key aspects highlighting the transformative effects of AI in the field of education:

Personalized Learning

- AI-driven adaptive learning platforms tailor educational content and pacing based on individual student needs and performance.
- Personalized learning ensures that students' progress at their own pace, receive targeted support, and master concepts before moving on.

Intelligent Tutoring Systems

- AI-powered tutoring systems provide real-time feedback and assis-

tance to students, offering additional support on specific topics or helping with homework.
- Intelligent tutoring systems adapt to each student's learning style, fostering a more effective and personalized learning experience.

Automated Grading and Feedback

- AI algorithms automate the grading process, saving teachers time and providing immediate feedback to students.
- Automated grading allows educators to focus on more nuanced aspects of teaching, such as facilitating discussions and addressing individual student needs.

Language Learning and Translation

- AI facilitates language learning through interactive platforms that adapt to individual proficiency levels and learning styles.
- Translation tools powered by AI support multilingual education, breaking down language barriers and promoting global collaboration.

Enhanced Educational Content Creation

- AI contributes to the creation of educational content, generating quizzes, interactive lessons, and simulations.
- Content creation tools powered by AI enable educators to develop engaging and diverse materials that cater to different learning preferences.

Predictive Analytics for Student Success

- AI analyzes student data to identify patterns and predict academic performance, allowing educators to intervene early and provide additional support.
- Predictive analytics help institutions implement targeted interventions to improve student retention and success rates.

Virtual Classrooms and Online Learning

- AI is integral to the development of virtual classrooms, offering immersive learning experiences through virtual reality (VR) and augmented reality (AR) technologies.
- Online learning platforms leverage AI for content recommendation, adaptive assessments, and intelligent course design.

Automated Administrative Tasks

- AI automates administrative tasks in educational institutions, including enrollment, scheduling, and resource allocation.
- Automation enhances operational efficiency, allowing administrative staff to focus on strategic planning and student support.

Facilitating Special Education

- AI tools assist in providing tailored support for students with special education needs, offering adaptive learning materials and personalized interventions.
- Assistive technologies powered by AI enhance accessibility and inclusivity in the learning environment.

Continuous Professional Development for Educators

- AI supports teachers' professional development by analyzing their teaching methods and providing insights for improvement.
- AI-driven professional development programs help educators stay abreast of pedagogical innovations and best practices.

While the impact of AI in education is substantial, ethical considerations, data privacy, and ensuring equitable access to AI-driven educational resources remain critical factors in the responsible implementation of these technologies. The evolving landscape of AI in education holds the potential to create more engaging, personalized, and effective learning experiences for students worldwide.

5

The Influence of AI on Employment and the Workplace

The impact of Artificial Intelligence (AI) on employment and work is multifaceted, presenting both challenges and opportunities as the technology continues to evolve. Here are key aspects highlighting the influence of AI on the job market and workplace:

Automation of Routine Tasks

- AI technologies, particularly robotic process automation (RPA), are capable of automating routine and repetitive tasks across various industries.
- Automation can lead to increased efficiency, reduced errors, and cost savings but may also result in job displacement for roles centered on repetitive tasks.

Creation of New Job Roles

- The implementation of AI often creates new job roles and opportunities, particularly in areas related to AI development, maintenance, and oversight.

- Emerging professions include AI specialists, data scientists, machine learning engineers, and ethicists focused on ensuring responsible AI use.

Enhanced Productivity and Efficiency

- AI tools improve workplace productivity by handling mundane tasks, allowing human workers to focus on more complex, creative, and value-added activities.
- Increased efficiency contributes to overall business growth and innovation.

Augmentation of Human Capabilities

- AI is designed to augment human capabilities rather than replace them entirely. Collaborative robots (cobots) work alongside human workers in industries such as manufacturing, healthcare, and logistics.
- Human-AI collaboration leverages the strengths of both, combining human creativity, emotional intelligence, and critical thinking with AI's analytical prowess.

Shift in Skill Requirements

- The rise of AI demands a shift in skill requirements, with an increased emphasis on skills such as data analysis, critical thinking, creativity, and adaptability.
- Lifelong learning becomes crucial as workers need to continuously update their skills to remain relevant in the changing job landscape.

Impact on Low-Skilled Jobs

- Routine and manual jobs are more susceptible to automation by AI, potentially impacting low-skilled workers.
- This shift underscores the importance of upskilling and reskilling initiatives to prepare the workforce for evolving job demands.

Job Displacement Concerns

- The automation of certain tasks may lead to concerns about job displacement in specific industries.
- Proactive measures, including workforce retraining programs and policies that address the social impact of automation, are essential to mitigate displacement effects.

AI in Decision-Making

- AI algorithms are increasingly used in decision-making processes, ranging from hiring practices to performance evaluations.
- Ethical considerations, transparency, and addressing biases in AI algorithms become critical to ensure fair and unbiased decision-making.

Flexible Work Arrangements

- AI facilitates the implementation of flexible work arrangements, including remote work and flexible schedules, improving work-life balance.
- Virtual assistants and AI-driven collaboration tools support seamless communication and collaboration in distributed work environments.

Economic Growth and Innovation

- AI contributes to economic growth by fostering innovation, creating new industries, and driving technological advancements.
- Investments in AI research and development spur job creation in technology-related fields and stimulate economic activity.

The impact of AI on employment and work is dynamic, influenced by factors such as the rate of AI adoption, regulatory frameworks, and societal responses. Addressing the challenges associated with AI in the workplace requires a comprehensive approach that includes education, workforce development, and thoughtful policy considerations to ensure a balanced and equitable future for the workforce.

6

The power of AI on the Finance Industry

T he impact of Artificial Intelligence (AI) on the finance industry is profound, revolutionizing the way financial institutions operate, make decisions, and interact with customers. Here are key aspects highlighting the influence of AI on finance:

Algorithmic Trading

- AI-driven algorithms analyze vast amounts of financial data in real-time, making split-second trading decisions to optimize investment portfolios.
- High-frequency trading (HFT) and algorithmic trading strategies leverage AI to detect market trends and execute trades with speed and precision.

Risk Management

- AI enhances risk assessment by analyzing historical data, identifying patterns, and predicting potential market fluctuations.
- Machine learning models contribute to more accurate risk evalua-

tions, allowing financial institutions to make informed decisions about investments and loans.

Fraud Detection and Security

- AI-powered fraud detection systems analyze transaction patterns, identify anomalies, and detect potentially fraudulent activities in real-time.
- Natural Language Processing (NLP) is used to monitor communication channels for signs of fraudulent behavior.

Customer Service and Chatbots

- AI-driven chatbots provide instant customer support, answer queries, and facilitate transactions, improving overall customer service efficiency.
- Virtual assistants powered by AI enhance user experiences in online banking, offering personalized recommendations and assistance.

Credit Scoring and Lending Decisions

- AI models analyze a wide range of data, including transaction history, social media activity, and non-traditional indicators, to assess creditworthiness.
- Automated credit scoring processes streamline lending decisions, leading to faster loan approvals and improved access to credit.

Personalized Financial Advice

- Robo-advisors use AI algorithms to provide personalized investment advice based on individual financial goals, risk tolerance, and market conditions.

- AI-driven financial planning tools help users optimize their investment portfolios and manage their finances more effectively.

Quantitative Analysis and Forecasting

- AI enables quantitative analysts to analyze market trends, assess investment opportunities, and forecast financial outcomes.
- Predictive analytics models powered by AI contribute to more accurate financial forecasting and decision-making.

Regulatory Compliance

- AI systems assist financial institutions in ensuring compliance with complex regulations by automating regulatory reporting and monitoring processes.
- Compliance-focused AI tools help identify potential risks and ensure adherence to industry standards and legal requirements.

Market Research and Sentiment Analysis

- AI tools analyze news articles, social media, and other sources to gauge market sentiment and identify potential market-moving events.
- Sentiment analysis contributes to more informed investment decisions and risk management strategies.

Operational Efficiency and Automation

- AI-driven automation streamlines back-office operations, reducing manual errors and increasing overall operational efficiency.

- Automation of routine tasks, such as data entry and reconciliation, allows financial professionals to focus on more strategic and complex activities.

The integration of AI in finance brings efficiency, innovation, and improved decision-making capabilities. However, it also raises ethical considerations, concerns about algorithmic biases, and the need for transparent and accountable AI systems. As the financial industry continues to embrace AI, finding a balance between innovation and responsible use is crucial for building trust and ensuring the long-term sustainability of AI applications in finance.

7

How AI is Reshaping Transportation

AI is fundamentally reshaping transportation by introducing innovative solutions that enhance safety, efficiency, and accessibility. In the realm of autonomous vehicles, AI powers self-driving cars, not only redefining the driving experience but also significantly improving safety through real-time data analysis and decision-making. Traffic management benefits from AI's ability to optimize traffic flow, minimizing congestion, and predicting maintenance needs for infrastructure.

Public transportation undergoes a transformation as AI optimizes scheduling, route planning, and resource allocation. This leads to improved accessibility, reduced waiting times, and enhanced operational efficiency. Overall, AI in transportation is revolutionizing the way we move, promising safer, more efficient, and accessible travel experiences for individuals and communities.

Autonomous vehicles

AI in self-driving cars

The integration of artificial intelligence (AI) in self-driving cars marks a revolutionary leap in transportation. These vehicles utilize advanced AI algorithms to interpret real-time data from sensors, cameras, and other sources, enabling them to navigate, make decisions, and respond to their environment without human intervention. This breakthrough not only redefines the driving experience but also holds the potential to transform entire transportation systems.

Improved safety and reduced accidents

One of the primary advantages of incorporating AI into self-driving cars is the significant improvement in safety. AI systems continuously analyze vast amounts of data, detect potential hazards, and make split-second decisions to avoid collisions. With enhanced reaction times and 360-degree awareness, self-driving cars aim to drastically reduce accidents, making roads safer for passengers and pedestrians alike.

Traffic management

AI for optimizing traffic flow

Traffic congestion is a common challenge in urban areas, leading to wasted time and increased emissions. AI plays a pivotal role in optimizing traffic flow by analyzing real-time data from various sources, including traffic cameras, GPS devices, and sensors. Smart algorithms predict traffic patterns, identify bottlenecks, and dynamically adjust signal timings to ensure a smoother flow of vehicles. This not only reduces congestion but also minimizes travel times and enhances overall road efficiency.

Predictive maintenance of transportation infrastructure

AI-driven predictive maintenance is a proactive approach to ensuring the longevity and reliability of transportation infrastructure. By analyzing data from sensors embedded in roads, bridges, and tunnels, AI algorithms can predict potential maintenance needs before issues arise. This predictive capability allows authorities to schedule maintenance tasks efficiently, minimizing disruptions, and ensuring that the transportation infrastructure remains in optimal condition.

Public transportation optimization

AI-based scheduling and route planning

Public transportation systems benefit significantly from AI-based scheduling and route planning. By analyzing historical data, passenger patterns, and real-time information, AI algorithms optimize bus and train schedules. This ensures that public transportation aligns with the demands of commuters, reduces waiting times, and enhances overall efficiency. Smart scheduling also contributes to resource optimization, making public transportation a more viable and attractive option for daily commuters.

Improved accessibility and efficiency

AI optimization extends beyond schedules to improve accessibility for passengers. Adaptive systems can dynamically adjust routes based on demand, ensuring that public transportation remains accessible to diverse communities. Additionally, AI enhances operational efficiency by predicting peak times, optimizing vehicle allocation, and offering real-time updates to passengers. This creates a more seamless and responsive public transportation experience, encouraging increased ridership and reducing reliance on individual vehicles.

8

Smart Cities: Enhancing Urban Living through AI Integration

I n the pursuit of sustainable urban development, smart cities leverage the power of Artificial Intelligence (AI) to transform key areas. This comprehensive summary explores how AI is revolutionizing energy efficiency, waste management, and public safety in the urban landscape.

Energy efficiency

AI in energy consumption monitoring:

The implementation of AI in energy consumption monitoring is a cornerstone of creating smart cities. AI algorithms analyze real-time data from smart meters, sensors, and infrastructure to monitor energy usage patterns. This data-driven approach allows cities to identify areas of high consumption, optimize energy distribution, and implement targeted strategies for reducing overall energy consumption. By providing insights into usage trends, AI contributes to sustainable practices and resource conservation.

Smart grids and AI-driven power distribution

Smart grids, enhanced by AI, form a critical component of energy-efficient smart cities. AI algorithms predict and manage energy demand, integrating renewable energy sources seamlessly. Smart grids utilize real-time data to balance supply and demand dynamically, optimizing power distribution and reducing wastage. This not only enhances reliability but also facilitates the integration of renewable energy, paving the way for a more sustainable and resilient energy infrastructure.

Waste management

AI for optimizing waste collection:

Waste management in smart cities benefits from AI-driven optimization. Smart sensors placed in waste bins collect data on fill levels, and AI algorithms analyze this information to optimize collection routes. By dynamically adjusting collection schedules based on real-time data, cities can minimize operational costs, reduce emissions, and enhance the overall efficiency of waste management services.

Recycling initiatives with AI: AI contributes to more effective recycling initiatives in smart cities. Machine learning algorithms can identify recyclable materials from waste streams with high precision. This enables automated sorting processes in recycling plants, improving the quality and quantity of recyclable materials. By leveraging AI in recycling initiatives, smart cities promote environmental sustainability and reduce the strain on landfills.

Public safety

AI-powered surveillance and emergency response systems

AI plays a crucial role in enhancing public safety through advanced surveillance systems. AI-powered cameras analyze video feeds in real-time, detecting anomalies and potential threats. Additionally, AI-driven emergency response systems can analyze patterns, assess the severity of incidents, and provide crucial information to first responders. This proactive approach improves overall public safety and emergency response effectiveness.

Predictive policing using AI algorithms

Predictive policing, empowered by AI algorithms, enhances law enforcement efforts in smart cities. By analyzing historical crime data and other relevant factors, AI predicts potential crime hotspots. Law enforcement agencies can deploy resources strategically, preventing crimes before they occur. This data-driven approach not only improves the efficiency of policing but also fosters a safer environment for residents in smart cities.

9

AI and Social Interaction

Social media platforms leverage AI to enhance user experiences. Content recommendation algorithms analyze user preferences and behavior, delivering personalized content and fostering more engaging online interactions.

AI in social media

Content recommendation algorithms

AI-driven content recommendation algorithms analyze user behavior and preferences, delivering personalized content tailored to individual interests. This not only keeps users engaged but also fosters a sense of connection by curating content that resonates with their unique tastes.

Personalized user experiences

AI contributes to personalized user experiences on social media platforms by understanding user preferences, behaviors, and interactions. This personalized touch enhances user satisfaction, making the digital social space more meaningful and enjoyable.

Language translation

Real-time translation services

AI facilitates seamless cross-language communication through real-time translation services. Language barriers are overcome as AI algorithms translate text or spoken words instantly, fostering global connections and enabling diverse communities to engage in meaningful conversations.

Cross-cultural communication facilitated by AI

AI transcends cultural and linguistic boundaries by promoting effective communication between individuals from different backgrounds. It ensures that the richness of diverse perspectives can be shared and understood, fostering a global community that thrives on inclusivity.

Virtual companionship

AI chatbots for mental health support

AI-powered chatbots play a crucial role in providing mental health support. These virtual companions offer empathetic conversations, provide resources, and assist users in managing stress or emotional challenges, contributing to improved mental well-being.

AI-driven social interaction platforms

Virtual spaces enhanced by AI facilitate social interactions by creating immersive and engaging environments. AI algorithms analyze user behavior to tailor interactions, making digital social platforms more dynamic, enjoyable, and conducive to meaningful connections.

In this era of digital interconnectedness, AI in social interaction not only augments our online experiences but also redefines the very nature of human connection. From personalized content curation to breaking language barriers and offering virtual companionship, AI continues to shape a more inclusive and interconnected world.

10

Ethical Considerations and Challenges

As Artificial Intelligence (AI) continues to weave its way into various aspects of our lives, a critical examination of its ethical implications becomes imperative. This exploration delves into key considerations and challenges, addressing the delicate balance between technological advancement and ethical responsibility.

Bias in AI algorithms

One of the foremost concerns in AI development is the potential for bias in algorithms. AI systems learn from data, and if that data carries biases, the AI may perpetuate or even exacerbate societal prejudices. Understanding and mitigating bias in AI algorithms is a complex challenge that demands ongoing scrutiny, transparency, and a commitment to fairness. This session aims to unravel the intricacies of bias in AI, exploring strategies for creating more equitable and unbiased AI systems.

Privacy concerns

As AI relies on vast datasets to make informed decisions, the issue of privacy looms large. This session delves into the ethical considerations surrounding the collection, storage, and utilization of personal data by AI systems. Striking a balance between the need for data-driven insights and protecting individuals' privacy is crucial for fostering trust in AI technologies. Participants will explore frameworks for responsible data usage and the implementation of privacy-preserving measures in AI applications.

Job displacement and unemployment

The integration of AI in various industries brings forth concerns about job displacement and the potential impact on employment. This session addresses the nuanced relationship between AI and the workforce, exploring how automation might reshape job roles. It also delves into strategies for mitigating negative impacts, such as reskilling and upskilling initiatives, and fostering a collaborative environment where humans and AI technologies complement each other. By navigating these challenges, we can strive for a future where AI contributes to economic growth without leaving segments of the workforce behind.

11

Future Trends

As we stand at the forefront of the AI revolution, envisioning the future requires a keen understanding of the trajectories shaping this dynamic field. This exploration encompasses key sessions that delve into future trends, shedding light on the advancements, integrations, and societal implications that will define the next frontier of AI.

Advancements in AI technology

Unveiling the latest breakthroughs and innovations, this session propels us into the cutting edge of AI technology. From strides in machine learning to developments in natural language processing and computer vision, participants will gain insights into the next wave of AI capabilities. By understanding the advancements that lie ahead, we can anticipate the transformative impact these technologies will have on industries, society, and our daily lives.

Integration of AI with other emerging technologies

The synergy between AI and other emerging technologies is a frontier ripe with possibilities. This session navigates the intricate web of connections between AI and technologies like blockchain, Internet of Things (IoT), and augmented reality. Participants will explore how these integrations amplify the capabilities of both AI and its technological counterparts, paving the way for new applications, industries, and collaborative ecosystems.

Societal implications and adaptability

As AI becomes more intertwined with the fabric of society, understanding its broader implications is paramount. This session examines the societal impacts of widespread AI adoption, addressing questions of ethics, accessibility, and inclusivity. By exploring strategies for ensuring responsible AI development and fostering adaptability at both individual and societal levels, participants will contribute to shaping a future where AI enhances our collective well-being.

Embark on this journey into the future of AI, where these sessions promise to be a beacon illuminating the path forward. By embracing the advancements, understanding the integrations, and navigating the societal implications, we can collectively forge a future where AI serves as a force for positive transformation.

12

Conclusion: Navigating the Future Landscape of AI

As we draw the curtains on our exploration of the multifaceted impact of AI across diverse domains, it is imperative to recapitulate the key points that have surfaced throughout this comprehensive guide. From the transformative role of AI in healthcare and education to its influence on employment, finance, transportation, smart cities, social interaction, and the challenges it poses, our journey has unveiled the profound ways AI is reshaping our world.

Recap of key points:

In conclusion, the impact of AI across various sectors is undeniable, and its potential for transformative change is immense. Let us recap the key points discussed in each domain.

In healthcare, AI has revolutionized diagnosis, treatment, and patient care. From early disease detection to personalized medicine, AI is enhancing healthcare outcomes and saving lives.

In education, AI is reshaping the learning experience. It offers personalized learning paths, adaptive assessments, and intelligent tutoring systems, empowering students, and educators alike.

When it comes to employment and the workplace, AI is playing a significant role. In recruitment, automated screening and AI-driven hiring decisions streamline the hiring process. Skill enhancement and retraining programs powered by AI ensure a workforce that can adapt to the changing job landscape. Workflow automation boosts productivity and efficiency.

The finance industry benefits from AI-powered solutions by providing personalized financial advice, automated investment strategies, and robust fraud detection measures. Customer service is also improved through AI-powered chatbots and virtual assistants.

Transportation is being transformed by AI with the advent of autonomous vehicles, optimized traffic management, and improved public transportation systems. This leads to increased safety, reduced congestion, and enhanced accessibility.

In smart cities, AI integration promotes energy efficiency through monitoring consumption and optimizing power distribution. Waste management is optimized, and public safety is enhanced through AI-powered surveillance and emergency response systems.

AI has also made an impact on social interaction, enabling personalized user experiences on social media platforms, real-time language translation services, and providing virtual companionship for mental health support.

While embracing AI, we must address ethical considerations and challenges. Bias in AI algorithms, privacy concerns, and job displacement are crucial issues that require careful attention and regulation.

Looking towards the future, advancements in AI technology will continue to drive innovation and transformation. Integration with other emerging technologies such as blockchain, IoT, and robotics will unlock even greater potential. However, societal implications and adaptability must be carefully considered to ensure that AI benefits all and does not exacerbate existing inequalities.

Envisioning a future with AI-driven improvements

As we look toward the future, the potential for AI-driven improvements is boundless. Personalized healthcare, adaptive learning, efficient recruitment, secure financial transactions, and seamless transportation are just glimpses of the positive transformations that lie ahead. Smart cities may evolve into beacons of sustainability and safety, while AI-enabled social interactions foster cross-cultural understanding and mental well-being.

Call to action for responsible AI development and usage

Amidst these promises, it is crucial to emphasize the ethical considerations and challenges that accompany the AI revolution. Bias in algorithms, privacy concerns, and the potential for job displacement demand our vigilant attention. As we stride into the future, a collective commitment to responsible AI development and usage becomes paramount. The ethical framework surrounding AI must be robust, ensuring fairness, transparency, and accountability in its deployment.

In conclusion, this guide serves as a roadmap through the transformative landscape of AI, offering insights, perspectives, and foresight into the domains it touches. The responsibility now lies with all stakeholders – developers, policymakers, businesses, and individuals – to collectively shape an AI-driven future that is not only technologically advanced but also ethically sound and socially beneficial. Let us embark on this journey with a commitment to harnessing the full potential of AI for the greater good of humanity.